MW00713452

Education, An Essay And Other Selections

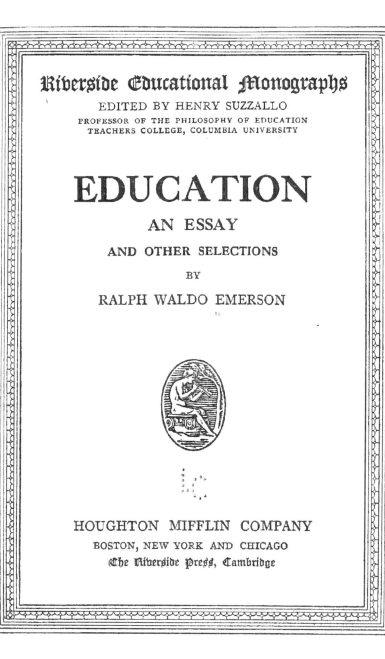

Riverside Educational Monographs

EDITED BY HENRY SUZZALLO

PROFESSOR OF THE PHILOSOPHY OF EDUCATION
TEACHERS COLLEGE, COLUMBIA UNIVERSITY

EDUCATION

AN ESSAY

AND OTHER SELECTIONS

BY

RALPH WALDO EMERSON

HOUGHTON MIFFLIN COMPANY

BOSTON, NEW YORK AND CHICAGO

The Riverside Press, Cambridge

EDITOR'S NOTE

The Riverside Educational Monographs

Modern education not fully apprehended

PROGRESS in educational theory has been so rapid in recent years, and changes in school-room practice have been made with such frequency, that many parents and teachers have failed to grasp the meaning of the new movements in education. This is not a matter for blame; it is characteristic of any period of transition such as ours As we have become conscious of the need of modifications in our school system to meet changing social conditions, we have attempted a welding of new ideals to old traditions, with the inevitable result that not a little waste and confusion have attended the administration of our schools.

As education grows scientific it tends to become less intelligible to the public

Fortunately, the significance of our modern education is constantly becoming clearer to those who are studying its problems and results in the light of the contributions from the fields of Psy-

iii

EDITOR'S NOTE

chology, Sociology, and Biology. More than ever before, educational theory and practice rest upon scientific truths. But as educational thought progresses it becomes increasingly difficult to keep leader, teacher, parent, and citizen in close contact. With a growing technical terminology, the educational thinker tends to speak in a dialect difficult for the ordinary person to comprehend ; and in addition, the educational specialist, to a larger extent than ever before, publishes his contributions in the proceedings of some learned society or in some other equally inaccessible place. The result is that as education has become more exact and scientific, it has tended to isolate itself from the understanding of people. It is necessary, therefore, that the thoughts of these leaders be transmitted to the rank and file —to all trainers of youth, to parents as well as to teachers. To meet this need, this series of Monographs is presented to the public with the hope that it may prove a contribution to the movement for a more general understanding of the progressive tendencies in American education.

The public must understand its schools

In a society such as ours, there are many reasons why educational institutions should be

EDITOR'S NOTE

popularly understood. Imperial edicts and bureaucratic decrees do not shape the spirit and method of our education. Each locality determines the particular form of organization of its schools, and the tacit agreement of the communities throughout the country gives the common stock of ideals which makes our teaching national in purpose.

Evidently then, it does not suffice that educational leaders alone should know the significance of a given reform or movement ; the public must also understand and accept the proposed policy. The intellectual channels between leader and follower, profession and populace, must be kept open. Then our schools will be guided in the spirit of our democratic institutions ; they will avoid unwise and unnecessary innovations, and necessary reforms will be more substantially achieved.

Intelligent parental cooperation needed

In the nineteenth century our people had an over-faith in the efficacy of school education. To-day, we have a better understanding of the limitations of the school. We have come to realize that the sphere of education embraces the whole of life, in school and out ; that many different agencies are required to make a cultured and efficient man. The school can do much, but there are aspects of life it cannot reach. The family has a rare power over the child, but it has special impotencies of its own.

Likewise other institutions offer but a partial training. It requires the cooperation of them all to develop the man of vision and power needed to-day. How, then, can the work of education be done unless others beside the teacher understand its aims and methods? Parents in particular must cooperate with the school if they would tide their children over moral and intellectual difficulties. And such cooperation requires the kind of understanding that comes not alone through sympathy, necessary as this is, but also through an acquaintance with the controlling and progressive tendencies in our education.

The education of teachers

It is probably true that the average teacher has none too clear an appreciation of much that is presented in our educational discussions. Indeed, it has been urged that there is a growing tendency for the superintendents of large and somewhat centralized systems of schools to make sweeping changes in school-room procedure without consulting, and, what is more serious, with-

EDITOR'S NOTE

out convincing the body of teachers of the necessity for such changes. If this be true, and there are certainly many evidences of such a tendency, then it indicates a serious fault which must be combated, for there can be no true profession of teaching where most of its members are required to carry out official orders mechanically. A clear understanding of underlying principles is essential to good teaching. Facts and methods are of little avail without this. In the art of ministering to the intellectual and moral crises of childhood so that strong free men shall be reared, the spiritual worker should fully comprehend the meaning of the plan. Fortunately, there are many practical leaders who realize that they must carry the teachers of the staff with them in all progressive reforms, not alone as a matter of respect for the teacher's personality, but as a matter of necessity in getting the high and subtle work of the school done. These will welcome any movement that will aid in the dissemination of the best professional knowledge and belief among the teachers of the country.

The scope of the Educational Monographs

To accomplish these large purposes, the volumes of this series are offered, the plan being

EDITOR'S NOTE

to present carefully selected writings upon education in convenient and attractive pocket editions at a smail cost. Usually but a single phase of education will be treated in a given number. The series will, however, finally include every aspect of our best educational thought, from the general statements of theory to the more specific and concrete details of school-room practice.

CONTENTS

INTRODUCTION

The worth of Emerson's views

THIS first volume of the Riverside Educational Monographs presents the views of Ralph Waldo Emerson regarding education. It consists of the entire essay on "Education," and several additional selections from his other writings. By no means a complete exposition of his philosophy of education, the material presents his fundamental beliefs with regard to the proper aims and methods which should be pursued in the liberal training of men and women. Written for the most part a generation ago, the subjects discussed are those which are of vital concern today. With rare penetration the essayist reveals the essential nature of the problems which everywhere arise in the effort to train free men.

A broad human training

In these days when we are necessarily so largely engaged in adding to our traditional education a system of specialized vocational training in the industrial, agricultural, and commercial arts, there is a danger that we shall lose our

INTRODUCTION

sense of proportion, forgetting the full significance of that older liberal education which is
designed to equip man for the finer uses of his
manhood and his citizenship.

There is no better brief for a broad, human
education than that presented in the writings of
Emerson. Our best American apostle of culture,
he notes with precision the qualities which are
the measure of a truly cultivated man. With high
critical power, he describes the futility and the
narrowness of much that goes under the guise
of human training in the schools, and ably de-
fends the larger cause of spiritual development,
despite the failures to achieve it in the class-
room. When sharp competition forces us to a
serious consideration of a school training for bread
winning, it is well to be told that the glorified
word efficiency means spiritual efficiency as much
as economic competency.

Men and nature as means

It is not alone in stating the need and the aim
of broad human training that these views of a
master mind are valuable. There is contributed
also a clear understanding of the means by which
men are to be cultivated. He points out that it
is not through books alone that men are to be

INTRODUCTION

educated. The basic training is to come through direct contact with things and men, — nature and society. Then books, interpreted by an experience-stocked imagination, will be more than words and dead languages. They will lift the student out of his own time and place to a larger and truer view of life through history, literature, and the other studies. The distinctly modern emphasis of nature study, manual work, play, and other social contacts as the foundation of a sound education, is just beginning to be realized in our school practice.

Teaching method as adjustment to the child

There is no better poised critic of our teaching methods than Emerson. He demonstrates clearly that the strenuous haste of the instructor to place a uniform coating of knowledge over the minds of children does not induce growth, and it cannot be called education. The child, as well as knowledge, needs to be understood. Human impulses, interests, and necessities, as well as subject matter, furnish the opportunities for the guidance of childhood The individuality of a child must be respected quite as much as the individuality of a fact. "Respect the child, respect him to the end, but also respect yourself. Be the com-

xiii

INTRODUCTION

panion of his thought, the friend of his friendship, the lover of his virtues, but no kinsman of his sin." Here is expressed all the naturalism of our modern education, but with no suggestion of its faults.

EDUCATION

I

EDUCATION

A NEW degree of intellectual power seems cheap at any price. The use of the world is that man may learn its laws. And the human race have wisely signified their sense of this, by calling wealth, means, — Man being the end. Language is always wise.

Therefore I praise New England because it is the country in the world where is the freest expenditure for education. We have already taken, at the planting of the Colonies (for aught I know for the first time in the world), the initial step, which for its importance might have been resisted as the most radical of revolutions, thus deciding at the start the destiny of this country, — this, namely, that the poor man, whom the law does not allow to take an ear of corn when starving, nor a pair of shoes for his freezing feet, is allowed to put his hand into the pocket of the rich, and say, You shall educate me, not as you will, but as I will : not alone in the elements, but, by further provision, in the languages, in sciences, in the useful and in elegant arts. The child shall be taken up by the State, and taught, at the public cost, the rudiments of knowledge, and at last, the ripest results of art and science.

Humanly speaking, the school, the college, society, make the difference between men. All the fairy tales of Aladdin or the invisible Gyges or the talisman that opens kings' palaces or the enchanted halls underground or in the sea, are only fictions to indicate the one miracle of intellectual enlargement. When a man stupid becomes a man inspired, when one and the same man passes out of the torpid into the perceiving state, leaves the din of trifles, the stupor of the senses, to enter into the quasi-omniscience of high thought, — up and down, around, all limits disappear. No horizon shuts down. He sees things in their causes, all facts in their connection.

One of the problems of history is the beginning of civilization. The animals that accompany and serve man make no progress as races. Those called domestic are capable of learning of man a few tricks of utility or amusement, but they cannot communicate the skill to their race. Each individual must be taught anew. The trained dog cannot train another dog. And Man himself in many races retains almost the unteachableness of the beast. For a thousand years the islands and forests of a great part of the world have been filled with savages who made no steps of advance in art or skill beyond the necessity of being fed and warmed. Certain nations, with a better brain and usually in more temperate climates, have made such progress as to compare with these as these compare with the bear and the wolf.

Victory over things is the office of man. Of course, until it is accomplished, it is the war and insult of things over him. His continual tendency, his great danger, is to overlook the fact that the world is only his teacher, and the nature of sun and moon, plant and animal only means of arousing his interior activity. Enamoured of their beauty, comforted by their convenience, he seeks them as ends, and fast loses sight of the fact that they have worse than no values, that they become noxious, when he becomes their slave.

This apparatus of wants and faculties, this craving body, whose organs ask all the elements and all the functions of Nature for their satisfaction, educate the wondrous creature which they satisfy with light, with heat, with water, with wood, with bread, with wool. The necessities imposed by this most irritable and all-related texture have taught Man hunting, pasturage, agriculture, commerce, weaving, joining, masonry, geometry, astronomy. Here is a world pierced and belted with natural laws, and fenced and planted with civil partitions and properties, which all put new restraints on the young inhabitant. He too must come into this magic circle of relations, and know health and sickness, the fear of injury, the desire of external good, the charm of riches, the charm of power. The household is a school of power. There, within the door, learn the tragi-comedy of human life. Here is the sincere thing, the wondrous composition for which day and night go round. In that routine are the sacred relations, the passions that bind and sever. Here is poverty and all the wisdom its hated necessities can teach, here labor drudges, here affections glow, here the secrets of character are told, the guards of man, the guards of woman, the compensations which, like angels of justice, pay every debt : the opium of custom, whereof all drink and many go mad. Here is Economy, and Glee, and Hospitality, and Ceremony, and Frankness, and Calamity, and Death, and Hope.

Every one has a trust of power, — every man, every boy a jurisdiction, whether it be over a cow or a rood of a potato-field, or a fleet of ships,

EDUCATION

or the laws of a state. And what activity the desire of power inspires! What toils it sustains! How it sharpens the perceptions and stores the memory with facts. Thus a man may well spend many years of life in trade. It is a constant teaching of the laws of matter and of mind. No dollar of property can be created without some direct communication with Nature, and of course some acquisition of knowledge and practical force It is a constant contest with the active faculties of men, a study of the issues of one and another course of action, an accumulation of power, and, if the higher faculties of the individual be from time to time quickened, he will gain wisdom and virtue from his business.

As every wind draws music out of the Æolian harp, so doth every object in Nature draw music out of his mind. Is it not true that every landscape I behold, every friend I meet, every act I perform, every pain I suffer, leaves me a different being from that they found me? That poverty, love, authority, anger, sickness, sorrow, success, all work actively upon our being and unlock for us the concealed faculties of the mind? Whatever private or petty ends are frustrated, this end is always answered Whatever the man does, or whatever befalls him, opens another chamber in his soul,—that is, he has got a new feeling, a new thought, a new organ. Do we not see how amazingly for this end man is fitted to the world?

What leads him to science? Why does he track in the midnight heaven a pure spark, a luminous patch wandering from age to age, but because he acquires thereby a majestic sense of power; learning that in his own constitution he can set the shining maze in order, and finding and carrying their law in his mind, can, as it were, see his simple idea realized up yonder in giddy distances and frightful periods of duration. If Newton come and first of men perceive that not alone certain bodies fall to the ground at a certain rate, but that all bodies in the Universe, the universe of bodies, fall always, and at one rate; that every atom in Nature draws to every other atom, —he extends the power of his mind not only over every cubic atom of his native planet, but he reports the condition of millions of worlds which his eye never saw. And what is the charm which every ore, every new plant, every new fact touching winds, clouds, ocean currents, the secrets of chemical composition and decomposition possess for Humboldt? What but that much revolving of similar facts in his mind has shown

EDUCATION

him that always the mind contains in its trans-
parent chambers the means of classifying the
most refractory phenomena, of depriving them
of all casual and chaotic aspect, and subordinat-
ing them to a bright reason of its own, and so
giving to man a sort of property, — yea, the
very highest property in every district and particle of the globe.

(By the permanence of Nature, minds are
trained alike, and made intelligible to each other.
In our condition are the roots of language and
communication, and these instructions we never
exhaust.)

In some sort the end of life is that the man
should take up the universe into himself, or out
of that quarry leave nothing unrepresented.
Yonder mountain must migrate into his mind.
Yonder magnificent astronomy he is at last to
import, fetching away moon and planet, solstice,
period, comet and binal star, by comprehending
their relation and law. Instead of the timid strip-
ling he was, he is to be the stalwart Archimedes,
Pythagoras, Columbus, Newton, of the physic,
metaphysic, and ethics of the design of the
world.

For truly the population of the globe has its
origin in the aims which their existence is to

7

serve ; and so with every portion of them. The truth takes flesh in forms that can express it ; and thus in history an idea always overhangs, like the moon, and rules the tide which rises simultaneously in all the souls of a generation.

Whilst thus the world exists for the mind ; whilst thus the man is ever invited inward into shining realms of knowledge and power by the shows of the world, which interpret to him the infinitude of his own consciousness, — it becomes the office of a just education to awaken him to the knowledge of this fact.

We learn nothing rightly until we learn the symbolical character of life. Day creeps after day, each full of facts, dull, strange, despised things, that we cannot enough despise, — call heavy, prosaic and desert. The time we seek to kill : the attention it is elegant to divert from things around us. And presently the aroused intellect finds gold and gems in one of these scorned facts, — then finds that the day of facts is a rock of diamonds ; that a fact is an Epiphany of God.

We have our theory of life, our religion, our philosophy ; and the event of each moment, the shower, the steamboat disaster, the passing of a beautiful face, the apoplexy of our neighbor, are all tests to try our theory, the approximate result we call truth, and reveal its defects. If I have renounced the search of truth, if I have come into the port of some pretending dogmatism, some new church or old church, some Schelling or Cousin, I have died to all use of these new events that are born out of prolific time into multitude of life every hour I am as a bankrupt to whom brilliant opportunities offer in vain. He has just foreclosed his freedom, tied his hands, locked himself up and given the key to another to keep.

When I see the doors by which God enters into the mind ; that there is no sot or fop, ruffian or pedant into whom thoughts do not enter by passages which the individual never left open, I can expect any revolution in character. " I have hope," said the great Leibnitz, "that society may be reformed, when I see how much education may be reformed."

It is ominous, a presumption of crime, that this word Education has so cold, so hopeless a sound. A treatise on education, a convention for education, a lecture, a system, affects us with slight paralysis and a certain yawning of the jaws. We are not encouraged when the law touches it with its fingers. Education should be as broad as man. Whatever elements are in him that should foster and demonstrate. If he be dexterous, his tuition should make it appear ; if he be capable of dividing men by the trenchant sword of his thought, education should unsheathe and sharpen it ; if he is one to cement society by his all-reconciling affinities, oh! hasten their action! If he is jovial, if he is mercurial, if he is great-hearted, a cunning artificer, a strong commander, a potent ally, ingenious, useful, elegant, witty, prophet, diviner, — society has need of all these. The imagination must be addressed. Why always coast on the surface and never open the interior of Nature, not by science, which is surface still, but by poetry? Is not the Vast an element of the mind? Yet what teaching, what book of this day appeals to the Vast?

Our culture has truckled to the times, — to the senses. It is not manworthy. If the vast and the spiritual are omitted, so are the practical and the moral. It does not make us brave or free. We teach boys to be such men as we are. We do not teach them to aspire to be all they can. We do not give them a training as if we believed in their noble nature. We scarce educate their bodies. We do not train the eye and the hand. We exercise their understandings to the apprehension and comparison of some facts, to a skill in numbers, in words ; we aim to make account- ants, attorneys, engineers ; but not to make able, earnest, great-hearted men. The great object of Education should be commensurate with the ob- ject of life. It should be a moral one ; to teach self-trust : to inspire the youthful man with an interest in himself ; with a curiosity touching his own nature ; to acquaint him with the resources of his mind, and to teach him that there is all his strength, and to inflame him with a piety towards the Grand Mind in which he lives. Thus would education conspire with the Divine Providence. A man is a little thing whilst he works by and for himself, but, when he gives voice to the rules of love and justice, is godlike, his word is current in all countries ; and all men, though his enemies, are made his friends and obey it as their own.

In affirming that the moral nature of man is the predominant element and should therefore be mainly consulted in the arrangements of a school, I am very far from wishing that it should swal- low up all the other instincts and faculties of man. It should be enthroned in his mind, but if it monopolize the man he is not yet sound, he does not yet know his wealth. He is in danger of becoming merely devout, and wearisome through the monotony of his thought. It is not less necessary that the intellectual and the active faculties should be nourished and matured. Let us apply to this subject the light of the same torch by which we have looked at all the phenomena of the time; the infinitude, namely, of every man. Everything teaches that.

One fact constitutes all my satisfaction, inspires all my trust, viz., this perpetual youth, which, as long as there is any good in us, we cannot get rid of. It is very certain that the coming age and the departing age seldom understand each other. The old man thinks the young man has no distinct purpose, for he could never get anything intelligible and earnest out of him. Perhaps the young man does not think it worth his while to explain himself to so hard and inapprehensive a confessor. Let him be led up with a long-sighted forbearance, and let not the sallies of his petulance or folly be checked with disgust or indignation or despair.

I call our system a system of despair, and I find all the correction, all the revolution that is needed and that the best spirits of this age promise, in one word, in Hope. Nature, when she sends a new mind into the world, fills it before-

EDUCATION

hand with a desire for that which she wishes it to know and do. Let us wait and see what is this new creation, of what new organ the great Spirit had need when it incarnated this new Will. A new Adam in the garden, he is to name all the beasts in the field, all the gods in the sky. And jealous provision seems to have been made in his constitution that you shall not invade and contaminate him with the worn weeds of your language and opinions. The charm of life is this variety of genius, these contrasts and flavors by which Heaven has modulated the identity of truth, and there is a perpetual hankering to violate this individuality, to warp his ways of thinking and behavior to resemble or reflect your thinking and behavior. A low self-love in the parent desires that his child should repeat his character and fortune; an expectation which the child, if justice is done him, will nobly disappoint. By working on the theory that this resemblance exists, we shall do what in us lies to defeat his proper promise and produce the ordinary and mediocre. I suffer whenever I see that common sight of a parent or senior imposing his opinion and way of thinking and being on a young soul to which they are totally unfit. Cannot we let people be themselves, and enjoy life in their own way? You are trying to make that man another *you.* One's enough.

Or we sacrifice the genius of the pupil, the unknown possibilities of his nature, to a neat and safe uniformity, as the Turks whitewash the costly mosaics of ancient art which the Greeks left on their temple walls. Rather let us have men whose manhood is only the continuation of their boyhood, natural characters still; such are able and fertile for heroic action; and not that sad spectacle with which we are too familiar, educated eyes in uneducated bodies.

I like boys, the masters of the playground and of the street, — boys, who have the same liberal ticket of admission to all shops, factories, armories, town-meetings, caucuses, mobs, target-shootings, as flies have; quite unsuspected, coming in as naturally as the janitor, — known to have no money in their pockets, and themselves not suspecting the value of this poverty; putting nobody on his guard, but seeing the inside of the show, — hearing all the asides. There are no secrets from them, they know everything that befalls in the fire-company, the merits of every engine and of every man at the brakes, how to work it, and are swift to try their hand at every part, so too the merits of every locomotive on the rails, and will coax the engineer to let them ride with him and pull the handle when it goes to the engine-house. They are there only for fun, and not knowing that they are at school, in the court-house, or the cattle-show, quite as much and more than they were, an hour ago, in the arithmetic class.

They know truth from counterfeit as quick as the chemist does. They detect weakness in your eye and behavior a week before you open your mouth, and have given you the benefit of their opinion quick as a wink. They make no mistakes, have no pedantry, but entire belief on experience. Their elections at baseball or cricket are founded on merit, and are right. They don't pass for swimmers until they can swim, nor for stroke-oar until they can row: and I desire to be saved from their contempt. If I can pass with them, I can manage well enough with their fathers.

Everybody delights in the energy with which boys deal and talk with each other; the mixture of fun and earnest, reproach and coaxing, love and wrath, with which the game is played;— the good-natured yet defiant independence of a leading boy's behavior in the school-yard. How we envy in later life the happy youths to whom

their boisterous games and rough exercise furnish the precise element which frames and sets
off their school and college tasks, and teaches
them, when least they think it, the use and
meaning of these. In their fun and extreme
freak they hit on the topmost sense of Horace.
The young giant, brown from his hunting-tramp,
tells his story well, interlarded with lucky allu-
sions to Homer, to Virgil, to college-songs, to
Walter Scott ; and Jove and Achilles, partridge
and trout, opera and binomial theorem, Cæsar in
Gaul, Sherman in Savannah, and hazing in Hol-
worthy, dance through the narrative in merry
confusion, yet the logic is good. If he can turn
his books to such picturesque account in his fish-
ing and hunting, it is easy to see how his reading
and experience, as he has more of both, will inter-
penetrate each other. And every one desires that
this pure vigor of action and wealth of narrative,
cheered with so much humor and street rhetoric,
should be carried into the habit of the young
man, purged of its uproar and rudeness, but with
all its vivacity entire. His hunting and campings-
out have given him an indispensable base : I wish
to add a taste for good company through his impatience of bad. That stormy genius of his needs
a little direction to games, charades, verses of

EDUCATION

society, song, and a correspondence year by year with his wisest and best friends Friendship is an order of nobility ; from its revelations we come more worthily into nature Society he must have or he is poor indeed ; he gladly enters a school which forbids conceit, affectation, emphasis, and dulness, and requires of each only the flower of his nature and experience ; requires good will, beauty, wit and select information ; teaches by practice the law of conversation, namely, to hear as well as to speak.

Meantime, if circumstances do not permit the high social advantages, solitude has also its lessons. The obscure youth learns there the practice instead of the literature of his virtues ; and, because of the disturbing effect of passion and sense, which by a multitude of trifles impede the mind's eye from the quiet search of that fine horizon-line which truth keeps, — the way to knowledge and power has ever been an escape from too much engagement with affairs and possessions ; a way, not through plenty and superfluity, but by denial and renunciation, into solitude and privation ; and, the more is taken away, the more real and inevitable wealth of being is made known to us. The solitary knows the essence of the thought, the scholar in society only its fair face. There is no want 'of example of great men, great benefactors, who have been monks and hermits in habit. The bias of mind is sometimes irresistible in that direction. The man is, as it were, born deaf and dumb, and dedicated to a narrow and lonely life. Let him study the art of solitude, yield as gracefully as he can to his destiny. Why cannot he get the good of his doom, and if it is from eternity a settled fact that he and society shall be nothing to each other, why need he blush so, and make wry faces to keep up a freshman's seat in the fine world? Heaven often protects valuable souls charged with great secrets, great ideas, by long shutting them up with their own thoughts. And the most genial and amiable of men must alternate society with solitude, and learn its severe lessons.

There comes the period of the imagination to each, a later youth; the power of beauty, the power of books, of poetry. Culture makes his books realities to him, their characters more brilliant, more effective on his mind, than his actual mates. Do not spare to put novels into the hands of young people as an occasional holiday and experiment; but, above all, good poetry in all kinds, epic, tragedy, lyric. If we can touch the imagination, we serve them, they will never forget it. Let him read Tom Brown at Rugby, read Tom Brown at Oxford, — better yet, read Hodson's Life — Hodson who took prisoner the king of Delhi. They teach the same truth, — a trust, against all appearances, against all privations, in your own worth, and not in tricks, plotting, or patronage.

I believe that our own experience instructs us that the secret of Education lies in respecting the pupil. It is not for you to choose what he shall know, what he shall do. It is chosen and foreordained, and he only holds the key to his own secret. By your tampering and thwarting and too much governing he may be hindered from his end and kept out of his own. Respect the child. Wait and see the new product of Nature. Nature loves analogies, but not repetitions. Respect the child. Be not too much his parent. Trespass not on his solitude

But I hear the outcry which replies to this suggestion : — Would you verily throw up the reins of public and private discipline ; would you leave the young child to the mad career of his own passions and whimsies, and call this anarchy a respect for the child's nature ? I answer, — Respect the child, respect him to the end, but

also respect yourself. Be the companion of his
thought, the friend of his friendship, the lover
of his virtue, — but no kinsman of his sin Let
him find you so true to yourself that you are the
irreconcilable hater of his vice and the imper-
turbable slighter of his trifling

The two points in a boy's training are, to keep
his *naturel* and train off all but that : — to keep
his *naturel*, but stop off his uproar, fooling and
horse-play ; — keep his nature and arm it with
knowledge in the very direction in which it
points. Here are the two capital facts, Genius
and Drill. The first is the inspiration in the well-
born healthy child, the new perception he has of
nature. Somewhat he sees in forms or hears in
music or apprehends in mathematics, or believes
practicable in mechanics or possible in political
society, which no one else sees or hears or believes. This is the perpetual romance of new life,
the invasion of God into the old dead world,
when he sends into quiet houses a young soul
with a thought which is not met, looking for
something which is not there, but which ought
to be there · the thought is dim but it is sure,
and he casts about restless for means and masters to verify it ; he makes wild attempts to explain himself and invoke the aid and consent of

EDUCATION

the bystanders. Baffled for want of language and
methods to convey his meaning, not yet clear to
himself, he conceives that though not in this
house or town, yet in some other house or town
is the wise master who can put him in possession
of the rules and instruments to execute his will.
Happy this child with a bias, with a thought
which entrances him, leads him, now into deserts,
now into cities, the fool of an idea. Let him fol-
low it in good and in evil report, in good or bad
company; it will justify itself; it will lead him
at last into the illustrious society of the lovers of
truth.

In London, in a private company, I became
acquainted with a gentleman, Sir Charles Fellowes, who, being at Xanthus, in the Ægean
Sea, had seen a Turk point with his staff to some
carved work on the corner of a stone almost
buried in the soil. Fellowes scraped away the
dirt, was struck with the beauty of the sculp-
tured ornaments, and, looking about him, ob-
served more blocks and fragments like this. He
returned to the spot, procured laborers and un-
covered many blocks. He went back to England, bought a Greek grammar and learned the
language; he read history and studied ancient
art to explain his stones; he interested Gibson

the sculptor; he invoked the assistance of the
English Government; he called in the succor of
Sir Humphry Davy to analyze the pigments; of
experts in coins, of scholars and connoisseurs;
and at last in his third visit brought home to
England such statues and marble reliefs and such
careful plans that he was able to reconstruct, in
the British Museum, where it now stands, the
perfect model of the Ionic trophy-monument,
fifty years older than the Parthenon of Athens,
and which had been destroyed by earthquakes,
then by iconoclast Christians, then by savage
Turks. But mark that in the task he had
achieved an excellent education, and become as-
sociated with distinguished scholars whom he
had interested in his pursuit; in short, had
formed a college for himself; the enthusiast had
found the master, the masters, whom he sought.
Always genius seeks genius, desires nothing so
much as to be a pupil and to find those who can
lend it aid to perfect itself.

Nor are the two elements, enthusiasm and
drill, incompatible. Accuracy is essential to
beauty. The very definition of the intellect is
Aristotle's: "that by which we know terms or
boundaries." Give a boy accurate perceptions.
Teach him the difference between the similar and

the same. Make him call things by their right
names. Pardon in him no blunder. Then he will
give you solid satisfaction as long as he lives. It
is better to teach the child arithmetic and Latin
grammar than rhetoric or moral philosophy, because they require exactitude of performance ; it
is made certain that the lesson is mastered, and
that power of performance is worth more than
the knowledge. He can learn anything which is
important to him now that the power to learn is
secured : as mechanics say, when one has learned
the use of tools, it is easy to work at a new craft.

Letter by letter, syllable by syllable, the child
learns to read, and in good time can convey to
all the domestic circle the sense of Shakspeare.
By many steps each just as short, the stammer-
ing boy and the hesitating collegian, in the school
debate, in college clubs, in mock court, comes at
last to full, secure, triumphant unfolding of his
thought in the popular assembly, with a fulness
of power that makes all the steps forgotten.

But this function of opening and feeding the
human mind is not to be fulfilled by any mechanical or military method ; is not to be trusted to
any skill less large than Nature itself. You must
not neglect the form, but you must secure the
essentials. It is curious how perverse and inter-

meddling we are, and what vast pains and cost we incur to do wrong. Whilst we all know in our own experience and apply natural methods in our own business, — in education our common sense fails us, and we are continually trying costly machinery against nature, in patent schools and academies, and in great colleges and universities.

The natural method forever confutes our experiments, and we must still come back to it. The whole theory of the school is on the nurse's or mother's knee. The child is as hot to learn as the mother is to impart. There is mutual delight. The joy of our childhood in hearing beautiful stories from some skilful aunt who loves to tell them, must be repeated in youth. The boy wishes to learn to skate, to coast, to catch a fish in the brook, to hit a mark with a snowball or a stone; and a boy a little older is just as well pleased to teach him these sciences. Not less delightful is the mutual pleasure of teaching and learning the secret of algebra, or of chemistry, or of good reading and good recitation of poetry or of prose, or of chosen facts in history or in biography.

Nature provided for the communication of thought, by planting with it in the receiving mind a fury to impart it. 'T is so in every art, in every science. One burns to tell the new fact,

EDUCATION

the other burns to hear it. See how far a young
doctor will ride or walk to witness a new surgical
operation. I have seen a carriage-maker's shop
emptied of all its workmen into the street, to
scrutinize a new pattern from New York. So in
literature, the young man who has taste for poetry, for fine images, for noble thoughts, is insa-
tiable for this nourishment and forgets all the
world for the more learned friend, — who finds
equal joy in dealing out his treasures.

(Happy the natural college thus self-instituted
around every natural teacher; the young men
of Athens around Socrates; of Alexandria around
Plotinus; of Paris around Abelard; of Germany
around Fichte, or Niebuhr, or Goethe: in short
the natural sphere of every leading mind) But
the moment this is organized, difficulties begin.
The college was to be the nurse and home of
genius; but, though every young man is born
with some determination in his nature, and is a
potential genius; is at last to be one, it is, in
the most, obstructed and delayed, and, whatever
they may hereafter be, their senses are now
opened in advance of their minds. They are
more sensual than intellectual. Appetite and
indolence they have, but no enthusiasm. These
come in numbers to the college: few geniuses:

and the teaching comes to be arranged for these
many, and not for those few. Hence the instruction seems to require skilful tutors, of accurate and systematic mind, rather than ardent and
inventive masters. Besides, the youth of genius
are eccentric, won't drill, are irritable, uncertain,
explosive, solitary, not men of the world, not good
for every-day association. You have to work for
large classes instead of individuals ; you must
lower your flag and reef your sails to wait for the
dull sailors ; you grow departmental, routinary,
military almost with your discipline and college
police But what doth such a school to form a great
and heroic character ? What abiding Hope can it
inspire ? What reformer will it nurse ? What poet
will it breed to sing to the human race? What dis-
coverer of Nature's laws will it prompt to enrich
us by disclosing in the mind the statute which all
matter must obey ? What fiery soul will it send out
to warm a nation with his charity ? What tran-
quil mind will it have fortified to walk with
meekness in private and obscure duties, to wait
and to suffer ? Is it not manifest that our aca-
demic institutions should have a wider scope;
that they should not be timid and keep the ruts
of the last generation, but that wise men thinking
for themselves and heartily seeking the good of

mankind, and counting the cost of innovation, should dare to arouse the young to a just and heroic life ; that the moral nature should be addressed in the school-room, and children should be treated as the high-born candidates of truth and virtue ?

So to regard the young child, the young man, requires, no doubt, rare patience : a patience that nothing but faith in the remedial forces of the soul can give. You see his sensualism ; you see his want of those tastes and perceptions which make the power and safety of your character. Very likely. But he has something else. If he has his own vice, he has its correlative virtue. Every mind should be allowed to make its own statement in action, and its balance will appear. In these judgments one needs that foresight which was attributed to an eminent reformer, of whom it was said, "his patience could see in the bud of the aloe the blossom at the end of a hundred years." Alas for the cripple Practice when it seeks to come up with the bird Theory, which flies before it. Try your design on the best school. The scholars are of all ages and temperaments and capacities. It is difficult to class them, some are too young, some are slow, some perverse. Each requires so much consideration, that the morning hope of the teacher, of a day of love and progress, is often closed at evening by despair. Each single case, the more it is considered, shows more to be done ; and the strict conditions of the hours, on one side, and the number of tasks, on the other. Whatever becomes of our method, the conditions stand fast, — six hours, and thirty, fifty, or a hundred and fifty pupils. Something must be done, and done speedily, and in this distress the wisest are tempted to adopt violent means, to proclaim martial law, corporal punishment, mechanical arrangement, bribes, spies, wrath, main strength and ignorance, in lieu of that wise genial providential influence they had hoped, and yet hope at some future day to adopt. Of course the devotion to details reacts injuriously on the teacher. He cannot indulge his genius, he cannot delight in personal relations with young friends, when his eye is always on the clock, and twenty classes are to be dealt with before the day is done. Besides, how can he please himself with genius, and foster modest virtue ? A sure proportion of rogue and dunce finds its way into every school and requires a cruel share of time, and the gentle teacher, who wished to be a Providence to youth, is grown a martinet, sore with suspicions ; knows as much vice as the judge of a police court, and his love of learning is lost in the routine of grammars and books of elements.

·A rule is so easy that it does not need a man to apply it , an automaton, a machine, can be made to keep a school so It facilitates labor and thought so much that there is always the temptation in large schools to omit the endless task of meeting the wants of each single mind, and to govern by steam. But it is at frightful cost Our modes of Education aim to expedite, to save labor , to do for masses what cannot be done for masses, what must be done reverently, one by one: say rather, the whole world is needed for the tuition of each pupil. The advantages of this system of emulation and display are so prompt and obvious, it is such a time-saver, it is so energetic on slow and on bad natures, and is of so easy application, needing no sage or poet, but any tutor or schoolmaster in his first term can apply it, — that it is not strange that this calomel of culture should be a popular medicine On the other hand, total abstinence from this drug, and the adoption of simple discipline and the following of nature, involves at once immense claims on the time, the thoughts, on the life of the teacher. It requires time, use, insight, event, all the great lessons and assistances of God; and only to think of using it implies character and profoundness; to enter on this course of discipline is to be good and great. It is precisely analogous to the difference between the use of corporal punishment and the methods of love. It is so easy to bestow on a bad boy a blow, overpower him, and get obedience without words, that in this world of hurry and distraction, who can wait for the returns of reason and the conquest of self; in the uncertainty too whether that will ever come? And yet the familiar observation of the universal compensations might suggest the fear that so summary a stop of a bad humor was more jeopardous than its continuance.

Now the correction of this quack practice is to import into Education the wisdom of life. Leave this military hurry and adopt the pace of Nature. Her secret is patience. Do you know how the naturalist learns all the secrets of the forest, of plants, of birds, of beasts, of reptiles, of fishes, of the rivers and the sea? When he goes into the woods the birds fly before him and he finds none; when he goes to the river-bank, the fish and the reptile swim away and leave him alone. His secret is patience; he sits down, and sits still ; he is a statue ; he is a log. These creatures have no value for their time, and he must put as low a rate on his. By dint of obstinate sitting still, reptile, fish, bird, and beast, which all wish to return to their haunts, begin to return. He sits still; if they approach, he remains passive as the stone he sits upon. They lose their fear. They have curiosity too about him. By and by the curiosity masters the fear, and they come swimming, creeping and flying towards him ; and as he is still immovable, they not only resume their haunts and their ordinary labors and manners, show themselves to him in their work-day trim, but also volunteer some degree of advances towards fellowship and good understanding with a biped who behaves so civilly and well. Can you not baffle the impatience and passion of the child by your tranquillity ? Can you not wait for him, as Nature and Providence do ? Can you not keep for his mind and ways, for his secret, the same curiosity you give to the squirrel, snake, rabbit, and the sheldrake and the deer ? He has a secret ; wonderful methods in him ; he is, — every child, — a new style of man ; give him time and opportunity. Talk of Columbus and Newton ! I tell you the child just born in yonder hovel is the beginning of a revolution as great as theirs. But you must have the believing and prophetic eye. Have the self-command you wish to inspire. (Your teaching and discipline must have the reserve and taciturnity of Nature. Teach them to hold their tongues by holding your own.) Say little ; do not snarl ; do not chide, but govern by the eye. See what they need, and that the right thing is done.

I confess myself utterly at a loss in suggesting particular reforms in our ways of teaching. No discretion that can be lodged with a school-committee, with the overseers or visitors of an academy, of a college, can at all avail to reach these difficulties and perplexities, but they solve themselves when we leave institutions and address individuals. The will, the male power, organizes, imposes its own thought and wish on others, and makes that military eye which controls boys as it controls men ; admirable in its results, a fortune to him who has it, and only dangerous when it leads the workman to overvalue and overuse it and precludes him from finer means. Sympathy, the female force, — which they must use who have not the first, — deficient in instant control and the breaking down of resistance, is more subtle and lasting and creative. I advise teachers to cherish mother-wit. I assume that you will

EDUCATION

keep the grammar, reading, writing, and arithmetic in order, 't is easy and of course you will. But smuggle in a little contraband wit, fancy, imagination, thought. If you have a taste which you have suppressed because it is not shared by those about you, tell them that. Set this law up, whatever becomes of the rules of the school : they must not whisper, much less talk ; but if one of the young people says a wise thing, greet it, and let all the children clap their hands. They shall have no book but school-books in the room ; but if one has brought in a Plutarch or Shakspeare or Don Quixote or Goldsmith or any other good book, and understands what he reads, put him at once at the head of the class. Nobody shall be disorderly, or leave his desk without permission, but if a boy runs from his bench, or a girl, because the fire falls, or to check some injury that a little dastard is inflicting behind his desk on some helpless sufferer, take away the medal from the head of the class and give it on the instant to the brave rescuer. If a child happens to show that he knows any fact about astronomy, or plants, or birds, or rocks, or history, that interests him and you, hush all the classes and encourage him to tell it so that all may hear. Then you have made your school-room like the world. Of course you will insist on modesty in the children, and respect to their teachers, but if the boy stops you in your speech, cries out that you are wrong and sets you right, hug him!

To whatsoever upright mind, to whatsoever beating heart I speak, to you it is committed to educate men. By simple living, by an illimitable soul, you inspire, you correct, you instruct, you raise, you embellish all. By your own act you teach the beholder how to do the practicable. According to the depth from which you draw your life, such is the depth not only of your strenuous effort, but of your manners and presence.

The beautiful nature of the world has here blended your happiness with your power. Work straight on in absolute duty, and you lend an arm and an encouragement to all the youth of the universe Consent yourself to be an organ of your highest thought, and lo! suddenly you put all men in your debt, and are the fountain of an energy that goes pulsing on with waves of benefit to the borders of society, to the circumference of things.

CULTURE IN EDUCATION

II

CULTURE IN EDUCATION

LET us make our education brave and preventive. Politics is an after-work, a poor patching. We are always a little late. The evil is done, the law is passed, and we begin the uphill agitation for repeal of that of which we ought to have prevented the enacting We shall one day learn to supersede politics by education. What we call our root-and-branch reforms of slavery, war, gambling, intemperance, is only medicating the symptoms. We must begin higher up, namely, in Education.

Our arts and tools give to him who can handle them much the same advantage over the novice, as if you extended his life ten, fifty, or a hundred years. And I think it the part of good sense to provide every fine soul with such culture, that it shall not, at thirty or forty years, have to say, "This which I might do is made hopeless through my want of weapons."

But it is conceded that much of our training fails of effect ; that all success is hazardous and rare ; that a large part of our cost and pains is thrown away. Nature takes the matter into her own hands, and, though we must not omit any jot of our system, we can seldom be sure that it has availed much, or that as much good would not have accrued from a different system.

Books, as containing the finest records of human wit, must always enter into our notion of culture. The best heads that ever existed, Pericles, Plato, Julius Cæsar, Shakspeare, Goethe, Milton, were well-read, universally educated men, and quite too wise to undervalue letters. Their opinion has weight, because they had means of knowing the opposite opinion. We look that a great man should be a good reader, or, in proportion to the spontaneous power, should be the assimilating power Good criticism is very rare, and always precious. I am always happy to meet persons who perceive the transcendent superiority of Shakspeare over all other writers. I like people who like Plato. Because this love does not consist with self-conceit.

But books are good only as far as a boy is ready for them. He sometimes gets ready very slowly. You send your child to the schoolmaster, but 't is the school-boys who educate him. You send him to the Latin class, but much of his tui-

tion comes, on his way to school, from the shop-
windows. You like the strict rules and the long
terms; and he finds his best leading in a by-way
of his own, and refuses any companions but of
his choosing. He hates the grammar and *Gradus*,
and loves guns, fishing-rods, horses, and boats.
Well, the boy is right; and you are not fit to
direct his bringing up, if your theory leaves out
his gymnastic training. Archery, cricket, gun
and fishing-rod, horse and boat, are all educators,
liberalizers; and so are dancing, dress, and the
street talk ; and — provided only the boy has resources, and is of a noble and ingenious strain —
these will not serve him less than the books. He
learns chess, whist, dancing, and theatricals. The
father observes that another boy has learned
algebra and geometry in the same time. But the
first boy has acquired much more than these
poor games along with them. He is infatuated
for weeks with whist and chess ; but presently
will find out, as you did, that when he rises from
the game too long played, he is vacant and for-
lorn, and despises himself. Thenceforward it
takes place with other things, and has its due
weight in his experience. These minor skills and
accomplishments, for example, dancing, are tick-
ets of admission to the dress-circle of mankind,

and the being master of them enables the youth to judge intelligently of much, on which, otherwise, he would give a pedantic squint. Landor said, "I have suffered more from my bad dancing, than from all the misfortunes and miseries of my life put together." Provided always the boy is teachable (for we are not proposing to make a statue out of punk), foot-ball, cricket, archery, swimming, skating, climbing, fencing, riding, are lessons in the art of power, which it is his main business to learn; — riding, specially, of which Lord Herbert of Cherbury said, "A good rider on a good horse is as much above himself and others as the world can make him." Besides, the gun, fishing-rod, boat, and horse constitute, among all who use them, secret freemasonries. They are as if they belonged to one club.

There is also a negative value in these arts. Their chief use to the youth is, not amusement, but to be known for what they are, and not to remain to him occasions of heartburn. We are full of superstitions. Each class fixes its eyes on the advantages it has not; the refined, on rude strength, the democrat, on birth and breeding. One of the benefits of a college education is, to show the boy its little avail. I knew a leading man in a leading city, who, having set his heart

on an education at the university, and missed it,
could never quite feel himself the equal of his
own brothers who had gone thither. His easy
superiority to multitudes of professional men
could never quite countervail to him this imagi-
nary defect. Balls, riding, wine-parties, and bil-
liards pass to a poor boy for something fine and
romantic, which they are not ; and a free admission to them on an equal footing, if it were possible, only once or twice, would be worth ten
times its cost, by undeceiving them.

Let me say here, that culture cannot begin
too early. In talking with scholars, I observe
that they lost on ruder companions those years
of boyhood which alone could give imaginative
literature a religious and infinite quality in their
esteem. I find, too, that the chance for appreciation is much increased by being the son of an
appreciator, and that these boys who now grow
up are caught not only years too late, but two or
three births too late, to make the best scholars
of. And I think it a presentable motive to a
scholar, that, as, in an old community, a well-
born proprietor is usually found, after the first
heats of youth, to be a careful husband, and to
feel a habitual desire that the estate shall suffer
no harm by his administration, but shall be de-

livered down to the next heir in as good condition as he received it ; — so, a considerate man will reckon himself a subject of that secular melioration by which mankind is mollified, cured, and refined, and will shun every expenditure of his forces on pleasure or gain, which will jeopard this social and secular accumulation.

The fossil strata show us that Nature began with rudimental forms, and rose to the more complex, as fast as the earth was fit for their dwelling-place ; and that the lower perish, as the higher appear. Very few of our race can be said to be yet finished men. We still carry sticking to us some remains of the preceding inferior quadruped organization. We call these millions men ; but they are not yet men. Half engaged in the soil, pawing to get free, man needs all the music that can be brought to disengage him. If Love, red Love, with tears and joy ; if Want with his scourge ; if War with his cannonade ; if Christianity with his charity ; if Trade with its money ; if Art with its portfolios ; if Science with her telegraphs through the deeps of space and time ; can set his dull nerves throbbing, and by loud taps on the tough chrysalis, can break its walls, and let the new creature emerge erect and free, — make way, and sing pæan! The age

CULTURE IN EDUCATION

of the quadruped is to go out, — the age of the brain and of the heart is to come in. The time will come when the evil forms we have known can no more be organized. Man's culture can spare nothing, wants all the material. He is to convert all impediments into instruments, all enemies into power. The formidable mischief will only make the more useful slave. And if one shall read the future of the race hinted in the organic effort of Nature to mount and meliorate, and the corresponding impulse to the Better in the human being, we shall dare affirm that there is nothing he will not overcome and convert, until at last culture shall absorb the chaos and gehenna. He will convert the Furies into Muses, and the hells into benefit.

EDUCATION FOR POWER

III

EDUCATION FOR POWER

THERE is not yet any inventory of a man's faculties, any more than a bible of his opinions. Who shall set a limit to the influence of a human being? There are men, who, by their sympathetic attractions, carry nations with them, and lead the activity of the human race. And if there be such a tie, that, wherever the mind of man goes, nature will accompany him, perhaps there are men whose magnetisms are of that force to draw material and elemental powers, and, where they appear, immense instrumentalities organize around them. Life is a search after power; and this is an element with which the world is so saturated, — there is no chink or crevice in which it is not lodged, — that no honest seeking goes unrewarded. A man should prize events and possessions, as the ore in which this fine mineral is found; and he can well afford to let events and possessions, and the breath of the body go, if their value has been added to him in the shape of power If he have secured the elixir, he can

47

spare the wide gardens from which it was distilled.
A cultivated man, wise to know and bold to perform, is the end to which nature works, and the
education of the will is the flowering and result
of all this geology and astronomy.

We must reckon success a constitutional trait.
Courage, — the old physicians taught (and their
meaning holds, if their physiology is a little
mythical), — courage, or the degree of life, is as
the degree of circulation of the blood in the
arteries. "During passion, anger, fury, trials of
strength, wrestling, fighting, a large amount of
blood is collected in the arteries, the maintenance of bodily strength requiring it, and but
little is sent into the veins. This condition is
constant with intrepid persons." Where the
arteries hold their blood, is courage and adven-
ture possible. Where they pour it unrestrained
into the veins, the spirit is low and feeble. For
performance of great mark, it needs extraordi-
nary health. If Eric is in robust health, and has
slept well, and is at the top of his condition, and
thirty years old, at his departure from Green-
land, he will steer west, and his ships will reach
Newfoundland. But take out Eric, and put in
a stronger and bolder man, — Biorn, or Thorfin,
— and the ships will, with just as much ease,

sail six hundred, one thousand, fifteen hundred miles farther, and reach Labrador and New England. There is no chance in results With adults, as with children, one class enter cordially into the game, and whirl with the whirling world; the others have cold hands, and remain bystanders; or are only dragged in by the humor and vivacity of those who can carry a dead-weight. The first wealth is health. Sickness is poor spirited, and cannot serve any one: it must husband its resources to live. But health or fulness answers its own ends, and has to spare, runs over, and inundates the neighborhoods and creeks of other men's necessities.

All power is of one kind, a sharing of the nature of the world. The mind that is parallel with the laws of nature will be in the current of events, and strong with their strength. One man is made of the same stuff of which events are made; is in sympathy with the course of things; can predict it. Whatever befalls, befalls him first; so that he is equal to whatever shall happen. A man who knows men, can talk well on politics, trade, law, war, religion. For, everywhere, men are led in the same manners.

The advantage of a strong pulse is not to be supplied by any labor, art, or concert. It is like the climate, which easily rears a crop, which no glass, or irrigation, or tillage, or manures, can elsewhere rival. It is like the opportunity of a city like New York, or Constantinople, which needs no diplomacy to force capital or genius or labor to it. They come of themselves, as the waters flow to it. So a broad, healthy, massive understanding seems to lie on the shore of unseen rivers, of unseen oceans, which are covered with barks, that, night and day, are drifted to this point. That is poured into its lap, which other men lie plotting for. It is in everybody's secret; anticipates everybody's discovery; and if it do not command every fact of the genius and the scholar, it is because it is large and sluggish, and does not think them worth the exertion which you do.

This affirmative force is in one, and is not in another, as one horse has the spring in him, and another in the whip. "On the neck of the young man," said Hafiz, "sparkles no gem so gracious as enterprise." Import into any stationary district, as into an old Dutch population in New York or Pennsylvania, or among the planters of Virginia, a colony of hardy Yankees, with seething brains, heads full of steam-hammer, pulley, crank, and toothed wheel, — and everything begins to shine with values. What enhancement to all the water and land in England, is the arrival of James Watt or Brunel! In every company, there is not only the active and passive sex, but in both men and women, a deeper and more important *sex of mind*, namely, the inventive or creative class of both men and women, and the uninventive or accepting class. Each *plus* man represents his set, and, if he have the accidental advantage of personal ascendency, — which implies neither more nor less of talent, but merely the temperamental or taming eye of a soldier or a schoolmaster (which one has, and one has not, as one has a black mustache and one a blond), then quite easily, and without envy or resistance, all his coadjutors and feeders will admit his right to absorb them. The merchant works by book-keeper and cashier; the lawyer's authorities are hunted up by clerks; the geologist reports the surveys of his subalterns; Commander Wilkes appropriates the results of all the naturalists attached to the Expedition; Thorwaldsen's statue is finished by stone-cutters; Dumas has journeymen; and Shakspeare was theatre-manager, and used the labor of many young men, as well as the playbooks.

There is always room for a man of force, and

he makes room for many. Society is a troop of
thinkers, and the best heads among them take the
best places. A feeble man can see the farms that
are fenced and tilled, the houses that are built.
The strong man sees the possible houses and
farms. His eye makes estates, as fast as the sun
breeds clouds.

When a new boy comes into school, when a
man travels, and encounters strangers every day,
or, when into an old club a new-comer is do-
mesticated, that happens which befalls, when a
strange ox is driven into a pen or pasture where
cattle are kept; there is at once a trial of strength
between the best pair of horns and the new-comer,
and it is settled thenceforth which is the leader.
So now, there is a measuring of strength, very
courteous, but decisive, and an acquiescence
thenceforward when these two meet. Each reads
his fate in the other's eyes. The weaker party
finds, that none of his information or wit quite
fits the occasion. He thought he knew this or
that · he finds that he omitted to learn the end of
it. Nothing that he knows will quite hit the mark,
whilst all the rival's arrows are good, and well
thrown. But if he knew all the facts in the ency-
clopædia, it would not help him : for this is an affair
of presence of mind, of attitude, of aplomb : the

opponent has the sun and wind, and, in every cast, the choice of weapon and mark; and, when he himself is matched with some other antagonist, his own shafts fly well and hit. 'T is a question of stomach and constitution. The second man is as good as the first, — perhaps better; but has not stoutness or stomach, as the first has, and so his wit seems over-fine or under-fine.

Health is good, — power, life, that resists disease, poison, and all enemies, and is conservative, as well as creative. Here is question, every spring, whether to graft with wax, or whether with clay; whether to whitewash, or to potash, or to prune; but the one point is the thrifty tree. A good tree, that agrees with the soil, will grow in spite of blight, or bug, or pruning, or neglect, by night and by day, in all weathers and all treatments. Vivacity, leadership, must be had, and we are not allowed to be nice in choosing. We must fetch the pump with dirty water, if clean cannot be had. If we will make bread, we must have contagion, yeast, emptyings, or what not, to induce fermentation into the dough: as the torpid artist seeks inspiration at any cost, by virtue or by vice, by friend or by fiend, by prayer or by wine. And we have a certain instinct, that where is great amount of life, though gross and peccant, it has its own checks and purifications, and will be found at last in harmony with moral laws.

We watch in children, with pathetic interest, the degree in which they possess recuperative force. When they are hurt by us, or by each other, or go to the bottom of the class, or miss the annual prizes, or are beaten in the game, — if they lose heart, and remember the mischance in their chamber at home, they have a serious check. But if they have the buoyancy and resistance that preoccupies them with new interest in the new moment, — the wounds cicatrize, and the fibre is the tougher for the hurt.

Success goes thus invariably with a certain *plus* or positive power : an ounce of power must balance an ounce of weight. And, though a man cannot return into his mother's womb, and be born with new amounts of vivacity, yet there are two economies, which are the best *succedanea* which the case admits. The first is, the stopping off decisively our miscellaneous activity, and concentrating our force on one or a few points ; as the gardener, by severe pruning, forces the sap of the tree into one or two vigorous limbs, instead of suffering it to spindle into a sheaf of twigs.

"Enlarge not thy destiny," said the oracle :

EDUCATION FOR POWER

"endeavor not to do more than is given thee in charge" The one prudence in life is concentration, the one evil is dissipation : and it makes no difference whether our dissipations are coarse or fine ; property and its cares, friends, and a social habit, or politics, or music, or feasting. Everything is good which takes away one plaything and delusion more, and drives us home to add one stroke of faithful work. Friends, books, pictures, lower duties, talents, flatteries, hopes, — all are distractions which cause oscillations in our giddy balloon, and make a good poise and a straight course impossible. You must elect your work ; you shall take what your brain can, and drop all the rest. Only so, can that amount of vital force accumulate, which can make the step from knowing to doing. No matter how much faculty of idle seeing a man has, the step from knowing to doing is rarely taken. 'T is a step out of a chalk circle of imbecility into fruitfulness. Many an artist, lacking this, lacks all : he sees the masculine Angelo or Cellini with despair. He, too, is up to Nature and the First Cause in his thought. But the spasm to collect and swing his whole being into one act, he has not. The poet Campbell said, that "a man accustomed to work was equal to any achievement he resolved on, and that, for himself, necessity, not inspiration, was the prompter of his muse."

Concentration is the secret of strength in politics, in war, in trade, in short, in all management of human affairs. One of the high anecdotes of the world is the reply of Newton to the inquiry, "how he had been able to achieve his discoveries." "By always intending my mind." Or if you will have a text from politics, take this from Plutarch : "There was, in the whole city, but one street in which Pericles was ever seen, the street which led to the market-place and the council-house. He declined all invitations to banquets, and all gay assemblies and company. During the whole period of his administration, he never dined at the table of a friend." Or if we seek an example from trade, — "I hope," said a good man to Rothschild, "your children are not too fond of money and business : I am sure you would not wish that." "I am sure I should wish that : I wish them to give mind, soul, heart, and body to business, — that is the way to be happy. It requires a great deal of boldness and a great deal of caution to make a great fortune, and when you have got it, it requires ten times as much wit to keep it. If I were to listen to all the projects proposed to me, I should ruin myself very soon. Stick to one business, young man. Stick to your brewery (he said this to young Buxton), and you will be the great brewer of London. Be brewer, and banker, and merchant, and manufacturer, and you will soon be in the Gazette."

Many men are knowing, many are apprehensive and tenacious, but they do not rush to a decision. But in our flowing affairs a decision must be made, — the best, if you can , but any is better than none. There are twenty ways of going to a point, and one is the shortest; but set out at once on one. A man who has that presence of mind which can bring to him on the instant all he knows, is worth for action a dozen men who know as much, but can only bring it to light slowly. The good Speaker in the House is not the man who knows the theory of parliamentary tactics, but the man who decides off-hand. The good judge is not he who does hair-splitting justice to every allegation, but who, aiming at substantial justice, rules something intelligible for the guidance of suitors The good lawyer is not the man who has an eye to every side and angle of contingency, and qualifies all his qualifications, but who throws himself on your part so heartily, that he can get you out of a scrape. Dr. Johnson said, in one of his flowing sentences : "Miserable beyond all names of wretchedness is that unhappy pair, who are doomed to reduce beforehand to the principles of abstract reason all the details of each domestic day. There are cases where little can be said, and much must be done."

The second substitute for temperament is drill, the power of use and routine. The hack is a better roadster than the Arab barb. In chemistry, the galvanic stream, slow, but continuous, is equal in power to the electric spark, and is, in our arts, a better agent. So in human action, against the spasm of energy, we offset the continuity of drill. We spread the same amount of force over much time, instead of condensing it into a moment. 'T is the same ounce of gold here in a ball, and there in a leaf. At West Point, Colonel Buford, the chief engineer, pounded with a hammer on the trunnions of a cannon, until he broke them off. He fired a piece of ordnance some hundred times in swift succession, until it burst. Now which stroke broke the trunnion ? Every stroke Which blast burst the piece ? Every blast. "*Diligence passe sens*," Henry VIII was wont to say, or, great is drill. John Kemble said that the worst provincial company of actors would go through a play better than the best amateur company. Basil Hall likes to show that the worst regular troops will beat the best volunteers. Practice is nine tenths. A course of mobs is good practice for orators. All the great speakers were bad speakers at first. Stumping it through England for seven years made Cobden a consummate debater. Stumping it through New England for twice seven trained Wendell Phillips. The way to learn German is, to read the same dozen pages over and over a hundred times, till you know every word and particle in them and can pronounce and repeat them by heart. No genius can recite a ballad at first reading, so well as mediocrity can at the fifteenth or twentieth reading. The rule for hospitality and Irish "help," is, to have the same dinner every day throughout the year. At last, Mrs. O'Shaughnessy learns to cook it to a nicety, the host learns to carve it, and the guests are well served. A humorous friend of mine thinks, that the reason why Nature is so perfect in her art, and gets up such inconceivably fine sunsets, is, that she has learned how, at last, by dint of doing the same thing so very often. Cannot one converse better on a topic on which he has experience, than on one which is new?

EMERSON

Men whose opinion is valued on 'Change, are only such as have a special experience, and off that ground their opinion is not valuable. " More are made good by exercitation, than by nature," said Democritus. The friction in nature is so enormous that we cannot spare any power. It is not question to express our thought, to elect our way, but to overcome resistances of the medium and material in everything we do. Hence the use of drill, and the worthlessness of amateurs to cope with practitioners. Six hours every day at the piano, only to give facility of touch; six hours a day at painting, only to give command of the odious materials, oil, ochres, and brushes. The masters say that they know a master in music, only by seeing the pose of the hands on the keys;—so difficult and vital an act is the command of the instrument. To have learned the use of the tools, by thousands of manipulations; to have learned the arts of reckoning, by endless adding and dividing, is the power of the mechanic and the clerk.

I remarked in England, in confirmation of a frequent experience at home, that, in literary circles, the men of trust and consideration, bookmakers, editors, university deans and professors, bishops, too, were by no means men of the largest literary talent, but usually of a low and ordinary intellectuality, with a sort of mercantile activity and working talent. Indifferent hacks and mediocrities tower, by pushing their forces to a lucrative point, or by working power, over multitudes of superior men, in Old as in New England.

I have not forgotten that there are sublime considerations which limit the value of talent and superficial success. We can easily overpraise the vulgar hero. There are sources on which we have not drawn. I know what I abstain from. But this force or spirit, being the means relied on by Nature for bringing the work of the day about, — as far as we attach importance to household life, and the prizes of the world, we must respect that. And I hold, that an economy may be applied to it; it is as much a subject of exact law and arithmetic as fluids and gases are; it may be husbanded, or wasted; every man is efficient only as he is a container or vessel of this force, and never was any signal act or achievement in history, but by this expenditure. This is not gold, but the gold-maker; not the fame, but the exploit.

If these forces and this husbandry are within reach of our will, and the laws of them can be read, we infer that all success, and all conceivable benefit for man, is also, first or last, within his reach, and has its own sublime economies by which it may be attained. The world is mathematical, and has no casualty, in all its vast and flowing curve. Success has no more eccentricity, than the gingham and muslin we weave in our mills. I know no more affecting lesson to our busy, plotting New England brains, than to go into one of the factories with which we have lined all the water-courses in the States. A man hardly knows how much he is a machine, until he begins to make telegraph, loom, press, and locomotive, in his own image. But in these, he is forced to leave out his follies and hindrances, so that when we go to the mill, the machine is more moral than we. Let a man dare go to a loom, and see if he be equal to it. Let machine confront machine, and see how they come out. The world-mill is more complex than the calico-mill, and the architect stooped less. In the gingham-mill, a broken thread or a shred spoils the web through a piece of a hundred yards, and is traced back to the girl that wove it, and lessens her wages. The stockholder, on being shown this, rubs his hands with delight. Are you so cunning, Mr. Profitloss, and do you expect to swindle your master and employer, in the web you weave?

EDUCATION FOR POWER

A day is a more magnificent cloth than any muslin, the mechanism that makes it is infinitely cunninger, and you shall not conceal the sleazy, fraudulent, rotten hours you have slipped into the piece, nor fear that any honest thread, or straighter steel, or more inflexible shaft, will not testify in the web.

THE TRAINING OF MANUAL
WORK

IV

THE TRAINING OF MANUAL
WORK

QUITE apart from the emphasis which the times
give to the doctrine, that the manual labor of
society ought to be shared among all the members, there are reasons proper to every individual, why he should not be deprived of it. The
use of manual labor is one which never grows
obsolete, and which is inapplicable to no person.
A man should have a farm or a mechanical craft
for his culture. We must have a basis for our
higher accomplishments, our delicate entertain-
ments of poetry and philosophy, in the work of
our hands. We must have an antagonism in the
tough world for all the variety of our spiritual
faculties, or they will not be born. Manual labor
is the study of the external world. The advantage of riches remains with him who procured
them, not with the heir. When I go into my
garden with a spade, and dig a bed, I feel such
an exhilaration and health, that I discover that I
have been defrauding myself all this time in let-
ting others do for me what I should have done

with my own hands. But not only health, but education is in the work. Is it possible that I who get indefinite quantities of sugar, hominy, cotton, buckets, crockery-ware, and letter-paper, by simply signing my name once in three months to a check in favor of John Smith & Co., traders, get the fair share of exercise to my faculties by that act, which nature intended for me in making all these far-fetched matters important to my comfort? It is Smith himself, and his carriers, and dealers, and manufacturers, it is the sailor, the hide-drogher, the butcher, the negro, the hunter, and the planter, who have intercepted the sugar of the sugar, and the cotton of the cotton. They have got the education, I only the commodity. This were all very well if I were necessarily absent, being detained by work of my own, like theirs, work of the same faculties; then should I be sure of my hands and feet, but now I feel some shame before my wood-chopper, my ploughman, and my cook, for they have some sort of self-sufficiency, they can contrive without my aid to bring the day and year round, but I depend on them, and have not earned by use a right to my arms and feet.

Consider further the difference between the first and second owner of property. Every species of property is preyed on by its own enemies, as iron by rust; timber by rot; cloth by moths; provisions by mould, putridity, or vermin; money by thieves; an orchard by insects; a planted field by weeds and the inroad of cattle; a stock of cattle by hunger; a road by rain and frost; a bridge by freshets. And whoever takes any of these things into his possession, takes the charge of defending them from this troop of enemies, or of keeping them in repair. A man who supplies his own want, who builds a raft or a boat to go a-fishing, finds it easy to calk it, or put in a thole-pin, or mend the rudder. What he gets only as fast as he wants for his own ends, does not embarrass him, or take away his sleep with looking after. But when he comes to give all the goods he has year after year collected, in one estate to his son, — house, orchard, ploughed land, cattle, bridges, hardware, wooden-ware, carpets, cloths, provisions, books, money, — and cannot give him the skill and experience which made or collected these, and the method and place they have in his own life, the son finds his hands full, — not to use these things, — but to look after them and defend them from their natural enemies. To him they are not means, but masters. Their enemies will not remit; rust, mould, vermin, rain, sun,

freshet, fire, all seize their own, fill him with vex-
ation, and he is converted from the owner into a
watchman or a watch-dog to this magazine of old
and new chattels. What a change! Instead of
the masterly good-humor, and sense of power, and
fertility of resource in himself ; instead of those
strong and learned hands, those piercing and
learned eyes, that supple body, and that mighty
and prevailing heart, which the father had, whom
nature loved and feared, whom snow and rain,
water and land, beast and fish, seemed all to know
and to serve, we have now a puny, protected person, guarded by walls and curtains, stoves and
down beds, coaches, and men-servants and wo-
men-servants from the earth and the sky, and
who, bred to depend on all these, is made anxious
by all that endangers those possessions, and is
forced to spend so much time in guarding them,
that he has quite lost sight of their original use,
namely, to help him to his ends, — to the prose-
cution of his love, to the helping of his friend, to
the worship of his God, to the enlargement of
his knowledge, to the serving of his country, to
the indulgence of his sentiment; and he is now
what is called a rich man, — the menial and run-
ner of his riches.

Hence it happens that the whole interest of

history lies in the fortunes of the poor. Knowledge, Virtue, Power, are the victories of man over his necessities, his march to the dominion of the world. Every man ought to have this opportunity to conquer the world for himself. Only such persons interest us, Spartans, Romans, Saracens, English, Americans, who have stood in the jaws of need, and have by their own wit and might extricated themselves, and made man victorious.

I do not wish to overstate this doctrine of labor, or insist that every man should be a farmer, any more than that every man should be a lexicographer. In general, one may say, that the husbandman's is the oldest, and most universal profession, and that where a man does not yet discover in himself any fitness for one work more than another, this may be preferred. But the doctrine of the Farm is merely this, that every man ought to stand in primary relations with the work of the world, ought to do it himself, and not to suffer the accident of his having a purse in his pocket, or his having been bred to some dishonorable and injurious craft, to sever him from those duties ; and for this reason, that labor is God's education; that he only is a sincere learner, he only can become a master, who learns the secrets of labor, and who by real cunning extorts from nature its sceptre.

Neither would I shut my ears to the plea of the learned professions, of the poet, the priest, the lawgiver, and men of study generally; namely, that in the experience of all men of that class, the amount of manual labor which is necessary to the maintenance of a family indisposes and disqualifies for intellectual exertion. I know it often, perhaps usually, happens, that where there is a fine organization apt for poetry and philosophy, that individual finds himself compelled to wait on his thoughts, to waste several days that he may enhance and glorify one; and is better taught by a moderate and dainty exercise, such as rambling in the fields, rowing, skating, hunting, than by the downright drudgery of the farmer and the smith. I would not quite forget the venerable counsel of the Egyptian mysteries, which declared that " there were two pairs of eyes in man, and it is requisite that the pair which are beneath should be closed, when the pair that are above them perceive, and that when the pair above are closed, those which are beneath should be opened." Yet I will suggest that no separation from labor can be without some loss of power and of truth to the seer himself ; that, I doubt not, the faults and vices of our literature and philosophy, their too great fineness, effeminacy, and melancholy, are attributable to the enervated and sickly habits of the literary class. Better that the book should not be quite so good, and the bookmaker abler and better, and not himself often a ludicrous contrast to all that he has written.

OUTLINE

I. EDUCATION

OUTLINE

II. CULTURE IN EDUCATION

III. EDUCATION FOR POWER

IV. THE TRAINING OF MANUAL LABOR

The Riverside Press
CAMBRIDGE . MASSACHUSETTS
U . S . A

Riverside Educational Monographs

Editor, HENRY SUZZALLO, Professor of The Philosophy of Education, Teachers College, Columbia University, New York.

NUMBERS READY OR IN PREPARATION

General Educational Theory

EDUCATION. An essay and other selections   By RALPH WALDO EMERSON   *Ready.*

THE MEANING OF INFANCY, and The Part Played by Infancy in the Evolution of Man. By JOHN FISKE.   *Ready*

EDUCATION FOR EFFICIENCY, and A New Definition of the Cultivated Man   By CHARLES W. ELIOT, President of Harvard University   *Ready.*

THE MORAL PRINCIPLES OF EDUCATION. By JOHN DEWEY, Professor of Philosophy, Columbia University   *Ready*

OUR NATIONAL IDEALS IN EDUCATION   By ELMER E. BROWN, United States Commissioner of Education   *In preparation.*

THE SCHOOL AS A SOCIAL INSTITUTION   By HENRY SUZZALLO, Professor of the Philosophy of Education, Teachers College, Columbia University.   *In preparation.*

Administration and Supervision of Schools

CONTINUATION SCHOOLS. By PAUL H HANUS, Professor of Education, Harvard University   *In preparation.*

CHANGING CONCEPTIONS OF EDUCATION   By E. P. CUBBERLY, Professor of Education, Leland Stanford Jr. University.
                                                       In preparation.

Methods of Teaching

SELF-CULTIVATION IN ENGLISH. By GEORGE HERBERT PALMER, Professor of Philosophy, Harvard University.   *Ready*

ETHICAL AND MORAL INSTRUCTION IN SCHOOLS. By GEORGE HERBERT PALMER, Professor of Philosophy, Harvard University
                                                          Ready

TEACHING CHILDREN TO STUDY   By LIDA B EARHART, Instructor in Elementary Education, Teachers College, Columbia University   *In preparation*

TYPES OF TEACHING. By FREDERIC ERNEST FARRINGTON, Associate Professor of Education, University of Texas   *In preparation*

Price 35 cents, each, net, postpaid

HOUGHTON MIFFLIN COMPANY

BOSTON   NEW YORK   CHICAGO